Rivers and Lakes

Mississippi River

John F. Prevost
ABDO Publishing Company

visit us at
www.abdopub.com

Published by ABDO Publishing Company, 4940 Viking Drive, Edina, Minnesota 55435.
Copyright © 2002 by Abdo Consulting Group, Inc. International copyrights reserved in
all countries. No part of this book may be reproduced in any form without written
permission from the publisher.

Printed in the United States.

Photo credits: Corbis

Contributing editors: Bob Italia, Tamara L. Britton, Kate A. Furlong, Kristin Van Cleaf
Book design and graphics: Neil Klinepier

Library of Congress Cataloging-in-Publication Data

Prevost, John F.
    Mississippi River / John Prevost.
      p. cm. -- (Rivers and lakes)
    Includes bibliographical references and index.
    Summary: Surveys the origin, geological borders, water, plant and
animal life, and economic and ecological aspects of the Mississippi
River.
    ISBN 1-57765-102-2
    1. Mississippi River--Juvenile literature. 2. Mississippi River
Valley--Juvenile literature. [1. Mississippi River.] I. Title.
II. Series.
F351.P68 1999
977--DC21   98-11984
                                           CIP
                                          AC

Contents

The Mississippi River 4

The River's Course 6

Plant Life 8

Animal Life 10

Climate 12

Native Cultures 14

Early Explorers 16

The Mississippi Today 18

The Environment 20

Glossary 22

How Do You Say That? 23

Web Sites 23

Index 24

The Mississippi River

*T*he Mississippi River is the largest river in North America. It travels 2,350 miles (3,781 km) from Minnesota to the Gulf of Mexico. It has rapids, falls, **floodplains**, and **wetland** marshes.

The Mississippi River's **source** is Lake Itasca in northern Minnesota. The Mississippi begins as a small stream only a few feet deep. As the river moves south, it collects rainwater and melted snow. Along the way, it also joins **tributaries** such as the Missouri, Ohio, and Arkansas Rivers. Together, they create a wide and muddy river.

The river and its banks are home to many kinds of plants and animals. People have used the river to travel and trade for hundreds of years. They have greatly altered the river. Today, many groups are working to preserve the river's natural environment.

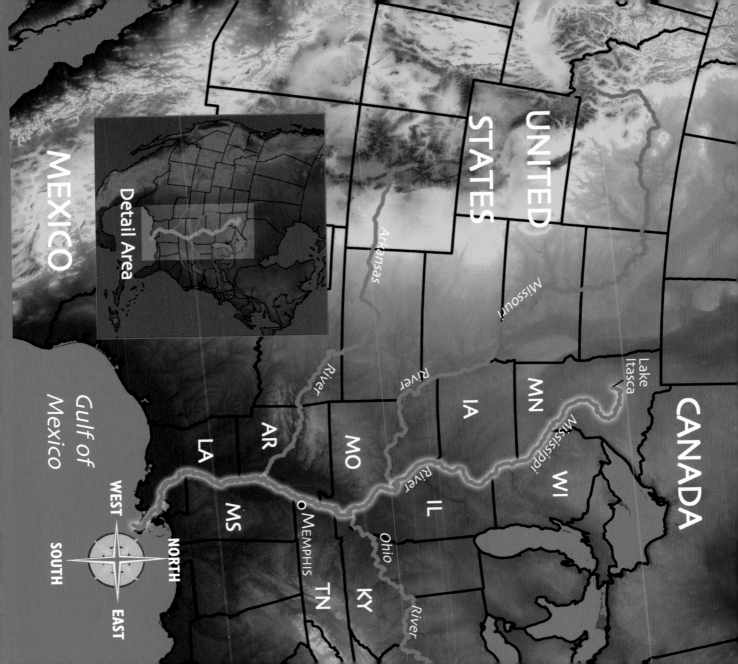

The River's Course

*T*he Mississippi River's path constantly changes. It flows through forests and plains. In the north, the force of the water cuts deep into the land to form **bluffs**.

As the Mississippi reaches the central plains, it loops back and forth. These curves are called meanders. Here the current moves fast. It **erodes** the land on its banks. Sometimes the current cuts through the land to meet itself again farther south. This creates small lakes and lagoons called oxbows along the river's shores.

In the south are the Mississippi's **floodplains**. In the spring, rain and melting snow flood the river. The water spills over the banks onto the floodplain. When the waters retreat, they leave behind **sediment** on the land. This creates rich soil, which helps **wetland** plants grow.

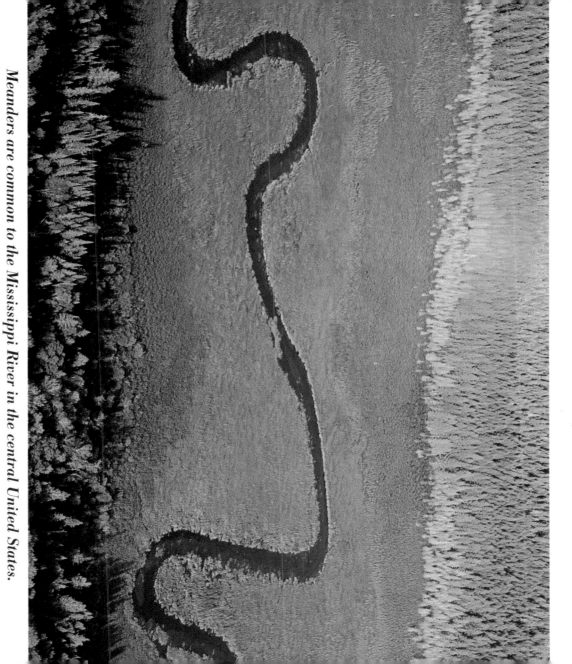

Meanders are common to the Mississippi River in the central United States.

Plant Life

Many kinds of plants are found in and around the Mississippi. They grow both in the river and along the shore. Tiny plants called phytoplankton grow in parts of the river where the current is slow and there is a lot of sunlight. Phytoplankton are too small to be seen without a microscope. They are a source of food for many small animals.

Larger plants grow along the banks of the Mississippi. In the north, trees such as pine, aspen, birch, and silver maple are abundant.

Many of the trees on the Mississippi's banks, such as the black willow, are **flood tolerant**. Black willows grow along the river's **floodplain**. They have adapted to benefit from the river's floods. Their roots can survive long periods under water. Branches break off in the flood. They root in the **sediment** left behind by the floodwaters.

Birch trees are common along the Mississippi's northern banks.

Animal Life

*T*he Mississippi River and its banks are home to many kinds of animals. Some live in the river's waters. Others live on the shore.

In the water, many of the animals are **invertebrates**. They are mostly insects, such as mayflies, stone flies, and caddis flies. Fish such as catfish, walleye, carp, smallmouth bass, and suckers live in the Mississippi, too.

Mammals such as beavers live on the **wetland** shore. These large rodents cut down trees to dam sections of the river. The dams turn the sections into large ponds. In the ponds, the beavers build tipi-shaped lodges. The ponds also provide homes for many other types of animals and plants.

The river and its valley are also an important flyway for migrating birds. Mallard ducks, Canada geese, songbirds, and birds of prey follow the river south for the winter.

Birds of prey, such as the bald eagle, depend on the Mississippi for food.

Climate

The Mississippi River affects the climate of the land around it. In the north, the flowing water warms the air and nearby land during the winter. In the south, the river cools the air and **floodplain**.

Land along the riverbanks experiences different types of weather. High humidity and fog are common along the river. Warm weather brings the chance of thunderstorms. On the **delta**, hurricanes can occur.

The river and its waters are a part of the hydrologic cycle. In the cycle, the sun heats the surface of a body of water. Some of the water **evaporates**. Wind carries it over land where it cools and falls as rain or snow. This moisture collects in streams and rivers where some of it returns to the Mississippi.

The Hydrologic Cycle

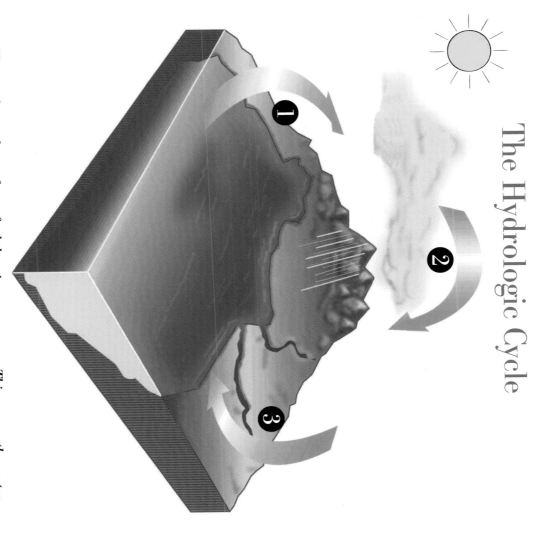

1. The sun heats the surface of a lake, river, or ocean. This causes the water to evaporate.

2. Wind carries the water vapor over land until it reaches a place where it begins to cool. The cooled water falls to the earth as rain or snow.

3. The rain and melted snow collect in streams. The streams carry the water to a lake, river, or ocean.

Native Cultures

Native Americans have lived along the Mississippi River for hundreds of years. They depended on the river. Many Native Americans traveled on the Mississippi in birch bark and dugout canoes. They also used the river for water and fishing.

During the 1600s, the Sioux was the most powerful tribe on the river's northern banks. Later, the Winnebago, Fox, Saux, and Ojibwa also moved there. The Ojibwa called the river *Messipi*, which means Big River. The river was also called *Mee-zee-see-bee*, which means Father of Waters.

Other Native American tribes lived along the river's southern banks. These tribes included the Choctaw, the Illinois, and the Chicasaw. They grew crops along the river's fertile shores.

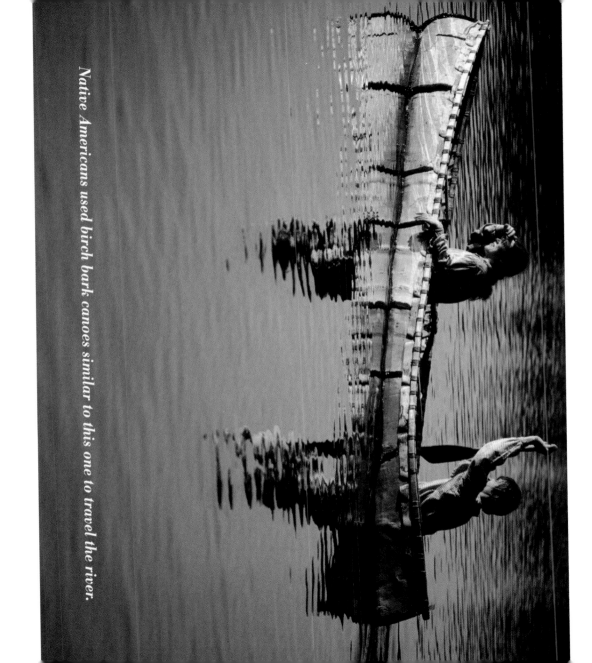

Native Americans used birch bark canoes similar to this one to travel the river.

Early Explorers

*E*uropeans first came to North America in the 1500s. In 1541, Spanish explorer Hernando de Soto was the first European to explore the Mississippi River. He and his men searched the river and its banks, looking for gold. They reached as far south as present-day Memphis, Tennessee.

In 1673, Frenchmen Louis Jolliet and Jacques Marquette explored the river. They traveled to the same point as de Soto before turning back. On their journey, they discovered that the river ran south. Until then, many people thought the river ran west.

Later, Rene-Robert de La Salle traveled the river with Henry de Tonty. In 1682, they became the first Europeans to reach the mouth of the river, at the Gulf of Mexico.

Jacques Marquette

The Mississippi Today

*T*oday, people still live along the Mississippi's banks. Cities and farms dot its shores. Ships traveling on the river carry goods. People use the river for boating and fishing.

People have changed the river in many useful ways. They have **dredged** the river to make it deeper. Dredging helps the shipping industry. The deeper water allows towboats and barges to haul products such as grain along the river.

People have built dams and **locks**. The dams create **reservoirs** for when the river level is low. Locks are used when the land rises too quickly. In the lock, the water level is raised or lowered to allow ships to pass from lower to higher land.

In the south, people have built levees along the river's **floodplain**. These high walls protect homes and farms by holding back the river's flood waters. Some levees are made of concrete. Others are made of earth with grass planted on top. The grass protects the levees from **erosion**.

18

How a Lock Works

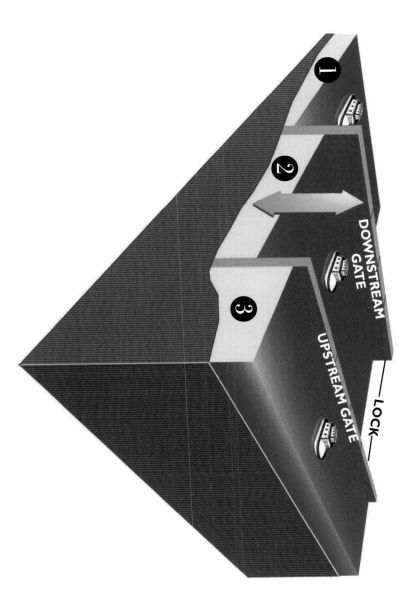

A ship traveling upstream enters the lock (1). The downstream gate closes behind it (2). Gravity pulls water from upstream into the lock. Water enters the lock until it is even with the water level upstream. The upstream gate opens and the ship moves out of the lock (3). This process is reversed if the ship is moving downstream.

The Environment

Not all of the changes people have made to the river are good. Chemical pollution from industries poisons the riverwater. This has **endangered** some plants and animals.

Farming has changed the riverbanks, too. Farmers cut down the trees to clear fields for planting. The trees once held the soil in place. Now, rain washes the soil into the river. This adds too much **sediment** into the river's water.

Dams trap the sediment, which used to travel with the riverwater. So people must **dredge** the river. But dredging puts excess sediment on the shores. This fills many of the oxbow lakes and **wetland** areas. So these areas can no longer absorb floodwater.

Levees and dams also stop the natural flooding that distributes sediment and replenishes the wetland marshes. Many wetlands have dried up, and many plants and animals have lost their homes.

Environmental groups are working to help the river. They want to restore the river's natural **ecosystems** while preserving homes and businesses.

Pollution from cities and industries has endangered the Mississippi.

Glossary

bluff - a high, steep bank or cliff.

delta - an area of land at the mouth of a river formed by the deposit of sediment, sand, and pebbles.

dredge - to make a waterway deeper. Machines are used to dredge rivers.

ecosystem - a community of organisms and their environment.

endangered - when all of a plant or animal species is in danger of dying out forever.

erosion - gradual wearing, rubbing, or washing away of the earth's rock or surface.

evaporate - to change from a liquid into a vapor.

floodplain - lowlands along a stream or river that are subject to flooding.

flood tolerant - able to survive being covered by water for a period of time.

invertebrate - an animal with no backbone.

lock - a closed space on a river with gates on each end. It is used to raise or lower boats to different water levels along the river.

reservoir - a natural or man-made place that stores water.

sediment - fine sand, clay, or soil carried by water that settles on the bottom of a river or lake.

source - a spring, lake, or other body of water where a river or stream begins.

tributary - a river or stream that flows into a larger river or stream.

wetland - land located in low areas that collects water and stays damp at least part of the year.

How Do You Say That?

hydrologic - hi-droh-LAH-jik
Illinois - ihl-ih-NOY
Jacques Marquette - JOK mahr-KET
Louis Jolliet - loo-EE juhwah-YAY
Ojibwa - oh-JIB-way
phytoplankton - fi-toh-PLANK-ten
reservoir - REZ-ehv-wahr
Rene-Robert de La Salle - ren-ay-roh-BEAR dee-la-sahl
Sioux - soo

Web Sites

Mississippi River Country
http://www.mississippi-river.com/mrc/
This site offers information on the river and the states along its banks. Each state has its own unique attractions, but they are all connected by the mighty Mississippi.

Ancient Architects of the Mississippi
http://www.cr.nps.gov/aad/feature
This site sponsored by the National Park Service contains information about ancient cultures along the river, traders and travelers, and a timeline.

These sites are subject to change. Go to your favorite search engine and type in Mississippi River for more sites.

Index

A

animals 4, 8, 10, 20
Arkansas River 4

B

bluffs 6

C

central plains 6
climate 12
current 6, 8

D

dams 10, 18, 20
de La Salle, Rene-
    Robert 16
de Soto, Hernando 16
de Tonty, Henry 16
delta 12
dredging 18, 20

E

environment 4, 20, 21
Europeans 16

F

farming 14, 18, 20
fish 10

floodplain 4, 6, 8, 12,
    18

G

Gulf of Mexico 4, 16

H

hydrologic cycle 12

I

industry 18, 20, 21
invertebrates 10
Itasca, Lake 4

J

Jolliet, Louis 16

L

levees 18, 20
locks 18

M

Marquette, Jacques 16
meanders 6
Missouri River 4

N

Native Americans 14
North America 4, 16

O

Ohio River 4
oxbow 6, 20

P

plants 4, 6, 8, 10, 20
pollution 20

R

reservoir 18

S

sediment 6, 8, 20
shipping 18

T

trade 4, 18
transportation 4, 14, 18
tributaries 4

W

weather 12
wetland 4, 6, 10, 20